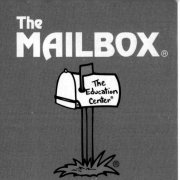

The MAILBOX®

Organize APRIL Now!™

...chool

Everything You Need for a Successful April

Monthly Organizing Tools
Manage your time, classroom, and students with monthly organizational tools.

Thematic Idea Collections
Practice essential skills this month with engaging activities and reproducibles.

April in the Classroom
Carry your monthly themes into every corner of the classroom.

Ready-to-Go Learning Centers and Skills Practice
Bring April to life right now!

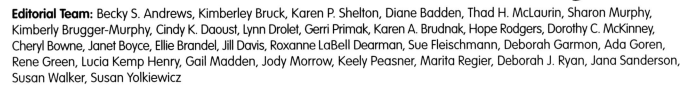

Managing Editor: Allison E. Ward

Editorial Team: Becky S. Andrews, Kimberley Bruck, Karen P. Shelton, Diane Badden, Thad H. McLaurin, Sharon Murphy, Kimberly Brugger-Murphy, Cindy K. Daoust, Lynn Drolet, Gerri Primak, Karen A. Brudnak, Hope Rodgers, Dorothy C. McKinney, Cheryl Bowne, Janet Boyce, Ellie Brandel, Jill Davis, Roxanne LaBell Dearman, Sue Fleischmann, Deborah Garmon, Ada Goren, Rene Green, Lucia Kemp Henry, Gail Madden, Jody Morrow, Keely Peasner, Marita Regier, Deborah J. Ryan, Jana Sanderson, Susan Walker, Susan Yolkiewicz

Production Team: Lisa K. Pitts, Pam Crane, Rebecca Saunders, Jennifer Tipton Cappoen, Chris Curry, Sarah Foreman, Theresa Lewis Goode, Clint Moore, Greg D. Rieves, Barry Slate, Donna K. Teal, Zane Williard, Tazmen Carlisle, Cat Collins, Marsha Heim, Amy Kirtley-Hill, Lynette Dickerson, Mark Rainey, Angela Kamstra, Debbie Shoffner

www.themailbox.com

Manufactured in the United States
10 9 8 7 6 5 4 3 2

Table of Contents

Monthly Organizing Tools
A collection of reproducible forms, notes, and other timesavers and organizational tools just for April.

Thematic Idea Collections
Fun, child-centered ideas for your favorite April themes.

April in the Classroom
In a hurry to find a specific type of April activity? It's right here!

Ready-to-Go Learning Centers and Skills Practice
Two center activities you can tear out and use today! Plus a collection of April-themed reproducibles for fine-motor skills practice!

Skills Grid

	Eggs	Rain	Pond	Bunnies	Centers	Circle Time & Games	Learning Center: Bunny's Crop	Learning Center: A Rainy Day	Ready-to-Go Skills Practice
Literacy									
syllables	18								
writing	19, 23			45					
interpreting directions	20								
matching letters	21	32							
matching letters in own name			34						
matching names					62				
prewriting		26							
associating /r/with r		29							
beginning sound /r/								82	
letter recognition			41						
rhyming				42					
sequencing				49					
letter formation					61				
Language Development									
listening				44					
following directions						67			
Math									
counting	19			43		67			
counting to 5							74		
patterns	21		35						
making sets	25		36						
number sets		27			62				
comparing sets		28							
matching sets		33							
identifying colors			37						
positional words				44					
one-to-one correspondence					60				
Science									
exploration		26							
scientific knowledge		28							
knowledge of environment			37						
animal habitat and behavior				43					
exploring living things						66			
Social & Emotional Development									
cooperation	20								
Physical Health & Development									
fine-motor skills		27							
gross-motor skills			36	45	61	66			
tracing									90, 91, 92
cut and glue									93, 94, 95, 96
Creative Arts									
movement	18								
dramatic play		29							
fine-motor skills			34						
participate in song			35						
using art media				42	60				

This is "egg-ceptional"!

_____   _____
date   teacher

©The Mailbox® • *Organize April Now!*™ • TEC60972

I'm Bursting With Good News!

Ask me!

©The Mailbox® • *Organize April Now!*™ • TEC60972

News "Splash"

©The Mailbox® • *Organize April Now!*™ • TEC60972

Awards: Use these awards to reinforce positive behaviors.

Headband

Glue to a construction paper strip sized to fit around a child's head.

Wristband

Tape the ends together where shown.

Medallion

Tape to a child's clothing or to a crepe paper necklace.

Headband, wristband, and medallion: Copy on colorful construction paper and use as desired.

April

Sunday	Monday	Tuesday	Wednesday	Thursday	Friday	Saturday

Center Checklist

Center

Name

Name

CLASS LIST

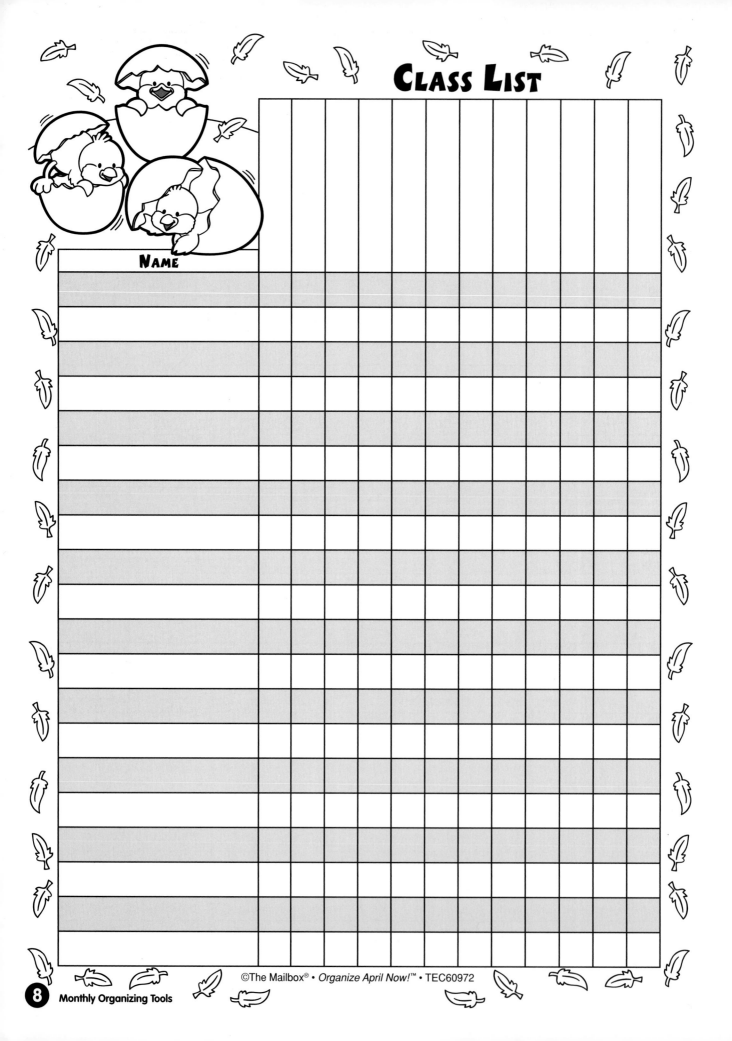

NAME										

Classroom News

From _____

Date _____

Help Wanted

Special Thanks

Look What We Are Learning

☆ Superstars

Please Remember

9

Classroom News

Date _____

From _____

Clip art: Use the artwork on student papers and on correspondence such as announcements, forms, and parent notes.

Materials to Collect:

Duties This Month:

Meetings:

Birthdays & special Dates:

Themes:

To Do:

- ◯
- ◯
- ◯
- ◯
- ◯
- ◯
- ◯
- ◯
- ◯
- ◯

Monthly planning form: Use this handy form to stay on top of April's school-related responsibilities.

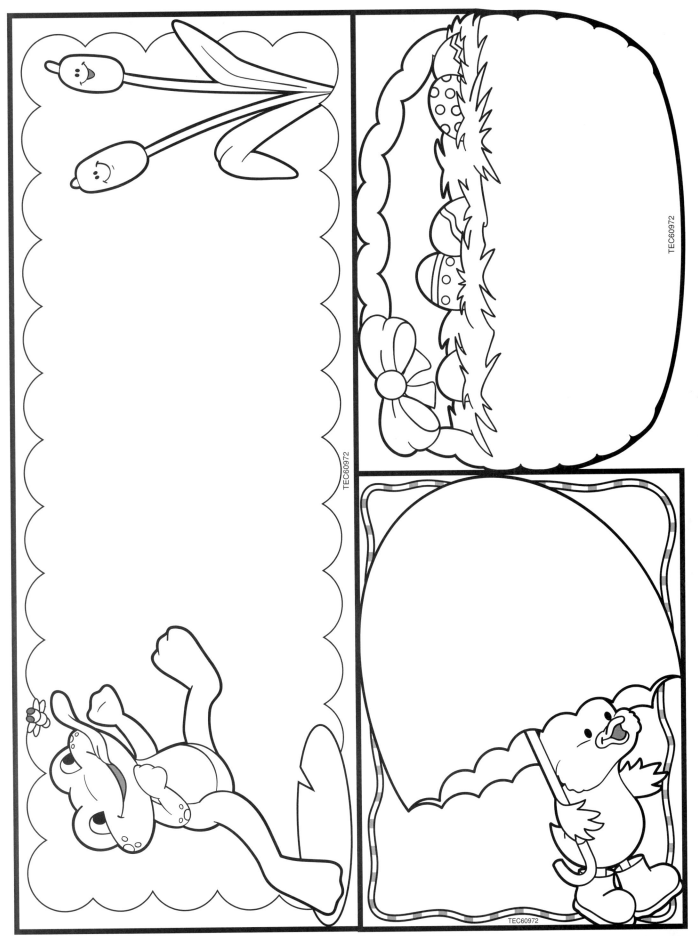

TEC60972

TEC60972

TEC60972

Table and cubby tags: Copy these tags on construction paper and personalize them with your youngsters' names. If desired, laminate the tags for durability.

Open: Use this page for parent correspondence or use it with students. For example, ask a child to draw herself dressed in rain gear. Then have her draw raindrops on the page.

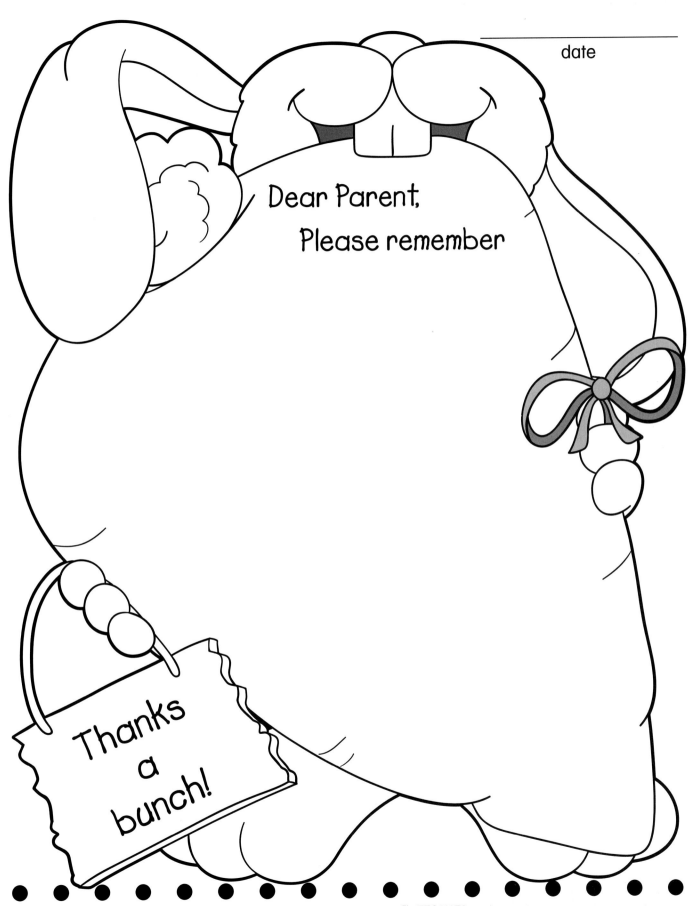

date

Dear Parent,

Please remember

Thanks a bunch!

Parent reminder note: Use this note to remind parents of supply requests, field trips, and special events such as classroom parties, school programs, or guest speakers.

School notes: Use these notes for parent communications such as announcing an upcoming event, requesting supplies or volunteers, and writing messages of praise.

No matter the weather, this family project will be loads of fun! Encourage your child to draw a picture on the raindrop of his or her favorite rainy-day activity. Help your child cut out the raindrop and then tell you about the activity as you write his or her thoughts on the back of the cutout.

We hope to see your project by _____.

Sincerely,

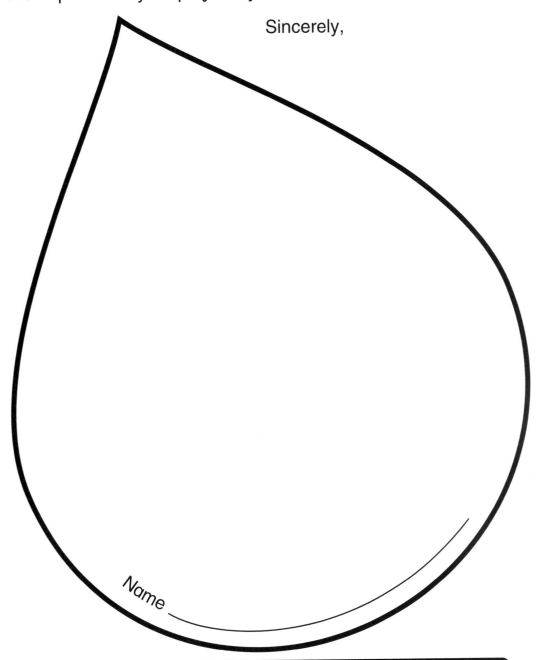

Name _____

Learning Links: develops fine-motor skills and prewriting skills

Note to the teacher: Date and sign a copy of the page; then make student copies on light blue construction paper. Write a child's name on the raindrop before sending it home with him. When he returns his project, invite him to share it with his classmates. Then post the raindrops on a display with the title "Rainy-Day Fun."

Eggs

No Yolks?

Students replace the missing yolks in this small-group activity. To prepare, cover a cookie sheet with aluminum foil to resemble a griddle. Then glue on eight egg white shapes. Also cut out a yellow construction paper copy of the yolks on page 22. Place the yolks and a spatula nearby. To begin, select a student to use the spatula to take an egg yolk. After he names the picture, have him repeat the word as you lead the group in clapping the word parts. If the word has one syllable, the child places the yolk onto an egg white. If it has two syllables, he sets it aside. Continue in this manner with additional student volunteers.

The Eggs Go Marching!

Little feet move to the beat with this egg-matching march! Gather a sheet of construction paper for every two students, each in a different color. Then cut two identical egg shapes from each sheet. Give one egg to every child. As you sing the song below, each child searches for her match. When she finds her twin, the two march behind you until all partners pair up successfully. For additional rounds, redistribute the eggs and play again.

(sung to the tune of "The Ants Go Marching")

The eggs go marching two by two. Hurrah! Hurrah!
The eggs go marching two by two. Hurrah! Hurrah!
Look around and you will see
An egg to match the one with thee.
And we'll all go marching around the room.
Hello, my friend!
Boom, boom, boom.

These "eggs-traordinary" cross-curricular activities are Grade A all the way!

Counting • • • • • • • • • • • • • • • • • • Math

Rolling for Eggs

Students enjoy collecting eggs at this partner center! To prepare, place a dozen plastic eggs in your sensory tub along with green shredded paper grass. Place a large die and a basket near the tub. To play, one child rolls the die. Her partner counts the dots, gathers the matching number of eggs, and places them in the basket. Students then switch roles and repeat the activity. To play again, the twosome returns the eggs to the tub, fluffs the grass, and rolls again. If desired, challenge older preschoolers to compare the egg sets using terms such as *more, less,* and *same number.*

Literacy • • • • • • • • • • • • • • • • • • Writing

Egg-Crackin' Animals

Little learners write about "egg-citing" animals as they discover that chickens are not the only animals that lay eggs! In advance, collect stuffed animals and pictures of egg-laying animals and place them in a box. Gather children and say that there are egg-laying critters hiding inside your mystery box. Then ask a volunteer to remove a critter from the box and help him identify it. Continue in this manner with additional volunteers until the box is empty. Next, help each child write his name on a copy of page 23. Then have him name his favorite egg-laying animal as you write the response to complete the sentence. To finish the page, have him illustrate the animal in the space provided.

The egg cracked open, and ___Keegan___ saw a ___dinosaur___
                            name

Egg-Laying Animals

dinosaur
turtle
alligator
snake
penguin
ostrich
duck
platypus

Cooperation

Goin' on an Egg Walk

To prepare for this partner activity, cut three large cracked egg halves from white construction paper. Place two cutouts side by side on the floor next to a chair and the third cutout on the chair. Invite a pair of students to walk on eggshells around the chair. To do this, each partner stands atop an eggshell. Partner 1 takes the third eggshell and places it in front of Partner 2 allowing her to move forward. Once Partner 2 moves, she picks up the shell she had been standing on and places it in front of Partner 1, paving the way for him to move forward. Partners continue taking turns moving forward around the chair until they reach their starting point.

Interpreting directions

Literacy

Designer Eggs

Youngsters enjoy filling decorative egg orders with this unique center idea! Make a variety of egg orders similar to the one shown. Using the egg colors on the orders, cut out several construction paper egg shapes. Place the eggs, orders, markers, and small paper bags at a center. To fill an order, a student uses the markers to make designs on the paper eggs to match the order card. When she is satisfied with her decorations, she uses the card to check her work as she puts the eggs in a bag. For a fun family connection, make the orders to go by sending the bags home to share.

Egg Order

Spots, Solids, and Stripes!

Little "eggs-perts" extend patterns at this jolly jumbo egg center! Cut out several colorful paper copies of the egg patterns on page 24. Prepare the patterns for students to copy and extend. Store the patterns and the eggs in a basket at a center. To participate, a child uses the eggs to copy and extend an egg pattern. For an added challenge, have youngsters create their own egg patterns.

Hide-and-Seek

Little ones will be eager to match and identify letters with this egg hunt. To prepare, place a magnetic letter in a plastic egg for each student. When youngsters are out of the classroom, hide the eggs and place an alphabet chart or strip in your large-group area. As students return, encourage them to hunt for the eggs. When a child finds an egg, he removes the letter from the egg and matches it to a letter on the alphabet chart. Once successful, he helps a classmate find an egg.

Find a reproducible activity on page 25.

Eggs 21

Egg Yolk Patterns
Use with "No Yolks?" on page 18.

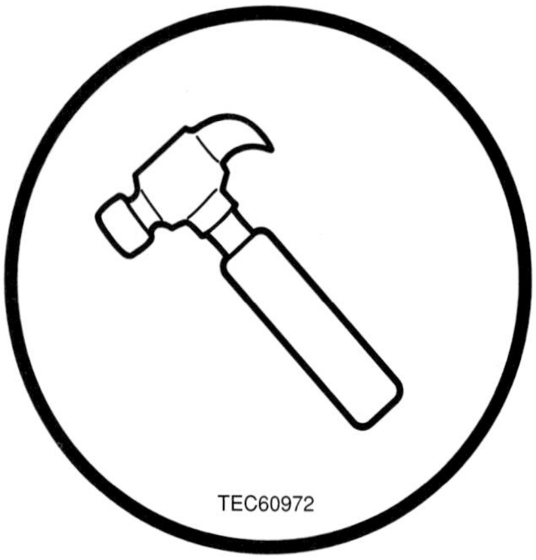

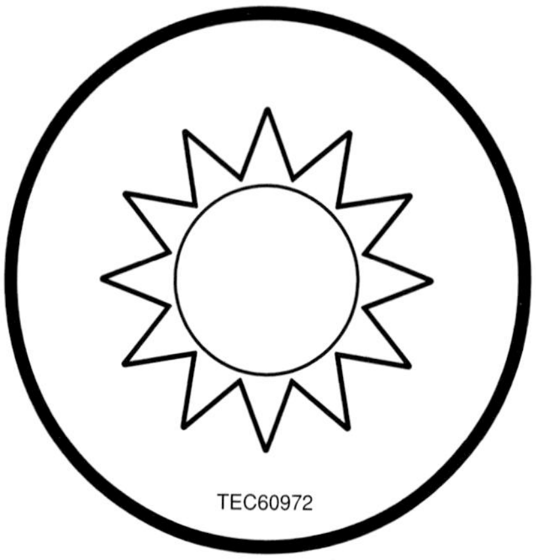

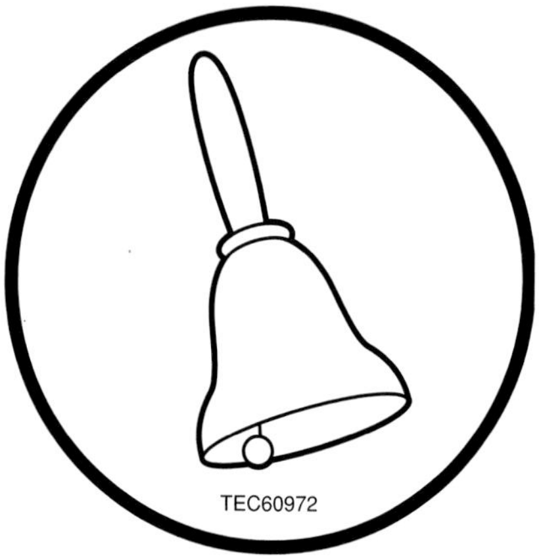

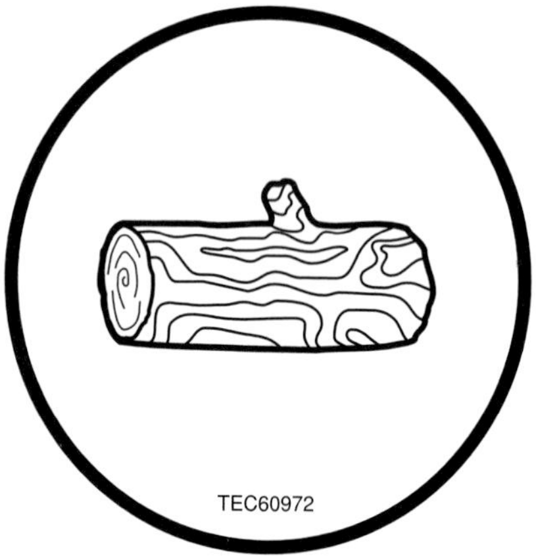

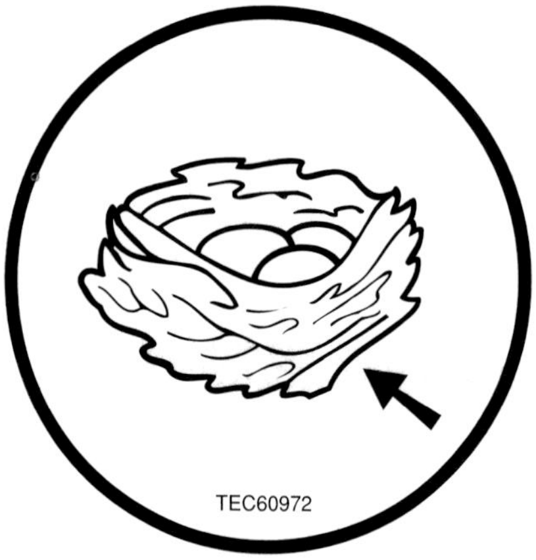

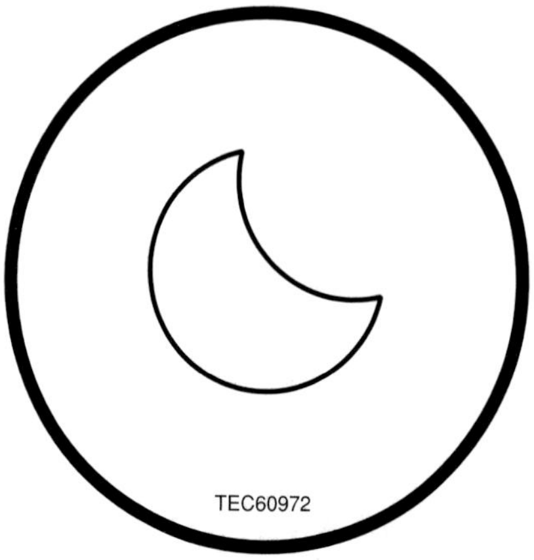

TEC60972

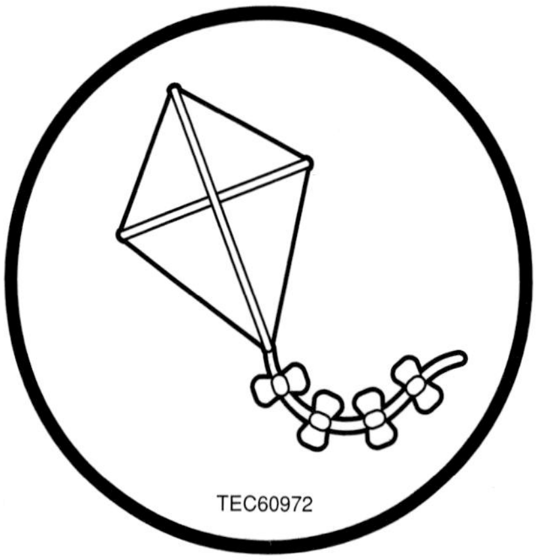

TEC60972

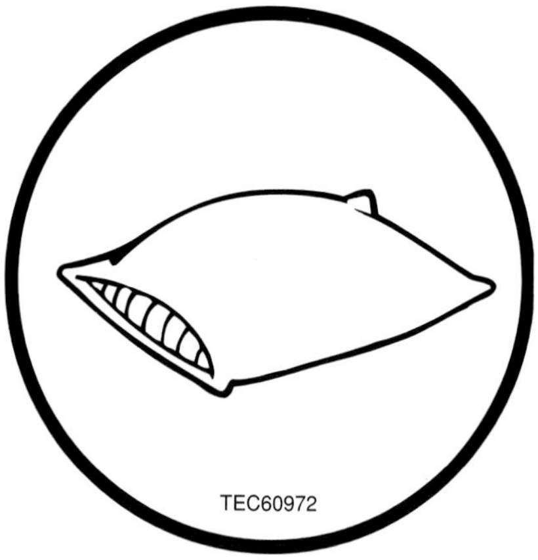

TEC60972

TEC60972

TEC60972

TEC60972

TEC60972

TEC60972

TEC60972

TEC60972

TEC60972

TEC60972

The egg cracked open, and

_____ saw a _____ .
name

Note to the teacher: Use with "Egg-Crackin' Animals" on page 19.

Writing | **23**

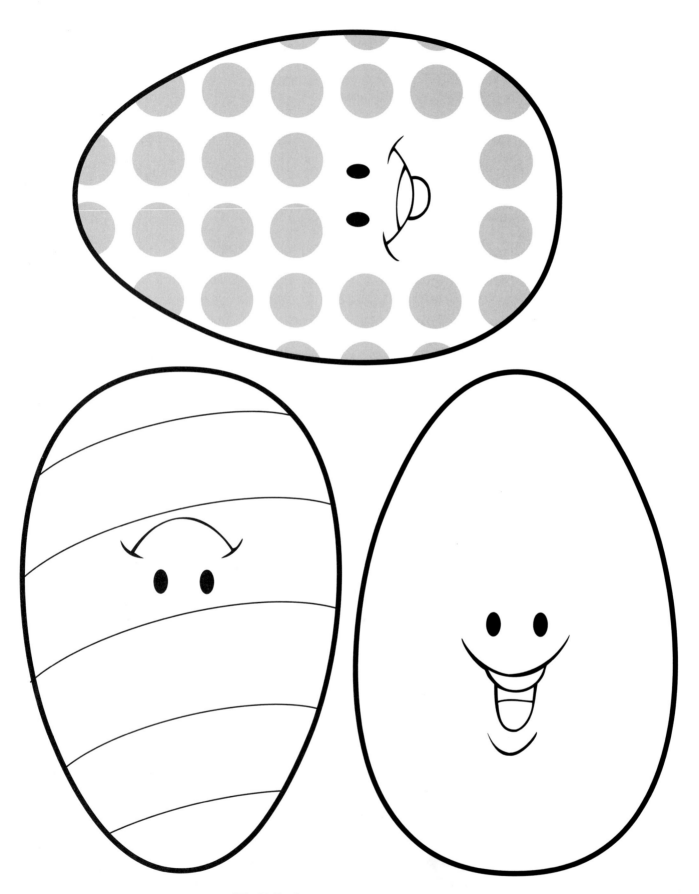

How Many Eggs?

Name _____

🖍 Draw eggs to match the number.

1	2
3	**4**

Rain

Science

Exploration

A Forecast of Rain

It's raining. It's pouring. Preschoolers are exploring—at the water table, that is! To prepare, gather several plastic containers in various sizes and shapes. Poke several holes in the bottom of each container, making sure each container's holes are a different size. Partially fill your water table with water and place the containers nearby. Invite little ones to visit the center, scoop water in the containers, and explore how rain falls. Encourage youngsters to describe the rain using terms such as *sprinkle, drizzle, shower,* and *downpour.*

Prewriting

Literacy

A Rainy Day Tale

For this class book project, encourage youngsters to name things that may get wet when it rains. Also ask them how some of these things could stay dry, making sure that an umbrella is mentioned. Then give each child a sheet of paper that you have programmed with the sentence starter "Rain falls on the _____." Write each child's dictated response in the blank and then invite her to draw a picture of that object getting wet in the rain.

To make the last page of the book, glue a class photo under a drawing of an umbrella and add the text "But it doesn't fall on us!" Stack students' papers atop the last page. Then bind the pages between two construction paper covers and add a title. Read the class book aloud, inviting each child to share her page. Youngsters are sure to be surprised when you read the last page!

But it doesn't fall on us!

Grab your galoshes and jump right into this downpour of learning activities!

Number sets • • • • • • • • • • • • • • • • • **Math**

Drip, Drop!

Raindrops fall into no-mess puddles at this center! To prepare, cut out several puddle shapes from blue construction paper and label each one with a different number. (For younger students, draw a dot set to represent each number.) Use the raindrop patterns on page 64 to make a supply of light blue raindrop cutouts. Place the raindrops and puddles at a center. When a child visits the center, he places a matching set of raindrops on each puddle.

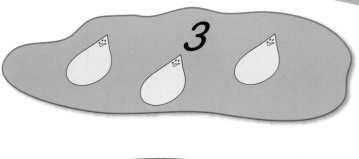

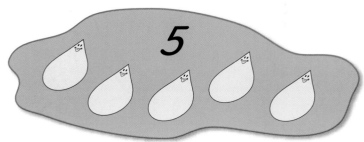

Physical Health & Development • • • • • • • • • • • *Fine-motor skills*

It's Raining!

This painting technique is sure to whip up a storm of excitement! For each child, use loops of masking tape to attach a construction paper umbrella cutout (pattern on page 63) to a sheet of gray construction paper. Place the prepared papers at a center along with containers of thinned blue paint and paintbrushes. A child dips a paintbrush in a container, holds it over her paper, and gently flicks the paintbrush so that the paint drops represent falling rain. She repeats the process using different colors. After the paint is dry, help her carefully remove the cutout to reveal an umbrella within a shower of colorful raindrops!

Amazing Rain

Help little ones learn about the importance of rain with this splashy song!

(sung to the tune of "The Wheels on the Bus")

The rain from the clouds helps flowers grow,
Flowers grow, flowers grow.
The rain from the clouds helps flowers grow
On a rainy day.

The rain from the clouds helps rivers flow,
Rivers flow, rivers flow.
The rain from the clouds helps rivers flow
On a rainy day.

The rain and the sun can make a rainbow,
Make a rainbow, make a rainbow.
The rain and the sun can make a rainbow,
On a rainy day.

Comparing sets • • • • • • • • • • • • • • • • Math

What's the Weather?

Whether the forecast calls for drizzle or a downpour, this whole-group activity showers youngsters with math practice! To prepare, write "more" on a card and "less" on another; then place the cards at opposite ends of a pocket chart. Cut out a copy of the cloudburst cards on page 30 and store them in a container.

In turn, invite two volunteers to each take a cloudburst card, count the raindrops aloud, and hold the card facing out toward the class. Lead the class in determining which card shows more raindrops and which card shows less. Then help each volunteer place his card under the appropriate heading in the pocket chart. Continue in the same manner, inviting different students to take a turn.

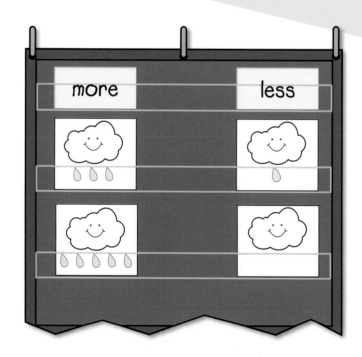

Dramatic play

Over in the Puddle

What better way to bring the outdoors in than with a rainy day dramatic-play center! Above the center, hang raindrop cutouts or blue lengths of crepe paper to resemble rain. Use clear Con-Tact covering to attach to the floor blue puddle cutouts and brown mud puddle cutouts. Place a box nearby filled with rain gear, such as raincoats, ponchos, and boots. Encourage center visitors to use the props to play in the rain without getting wet!

Creative Arts

Literacy

Associating /r/ with r

Raindrop Roundup

Little ones collect raindrops during this circle-time activity! Cut out a construction paper copy of the raindrop pictures on page 31. Place the raindrops in a white paper lunch bag to represent a cloud. Seat youngsters in a circle. Lead students in singing the song shown as they pass around the cloud. When the verse is complete, ask the child holding the cloud to remove a raindrop and name the picture. Then invite all of the students to repeat the word, emphasizing the /r/ sound. Continue in the same manner until each raindrop has "fallen" from the cloud!

(sung to the tune of "Mary Had a Little Lamb")

Pass the rain cloud round and round,
Round and round, round and round.
Pass the rain cloud round and round;
Then listen for the /r/ sound!

Find reproducible activities on pages 32–33.

Cloudbursts Cards

Use with "What's the Weather?" on page 28.

TEC60972

TEC60972

TEC60972

TEC60972

TEC60972

TEC60972

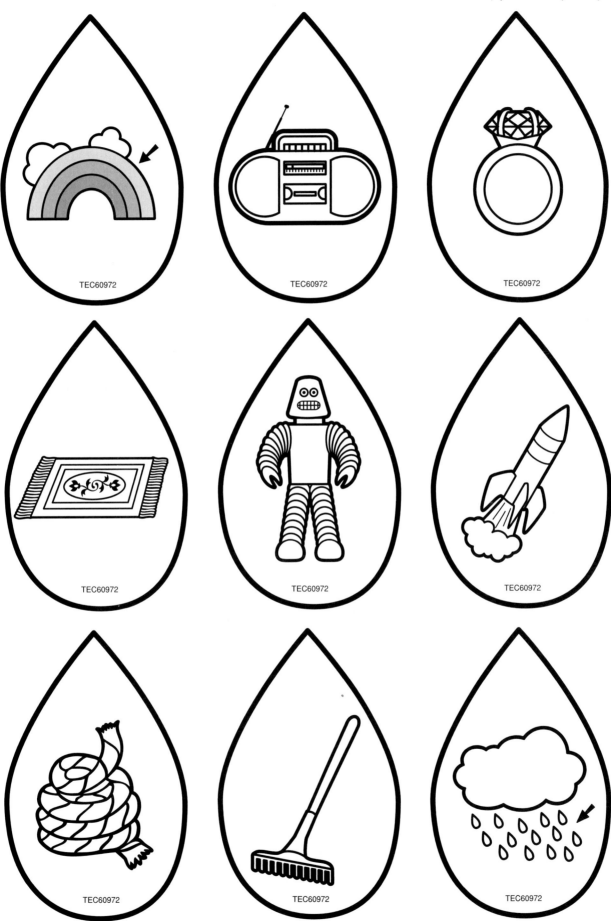

In the Clouds

Name _____

🖍 Color the raindrops that match the cloud.

Matching Letters

Rain Day

Name _____

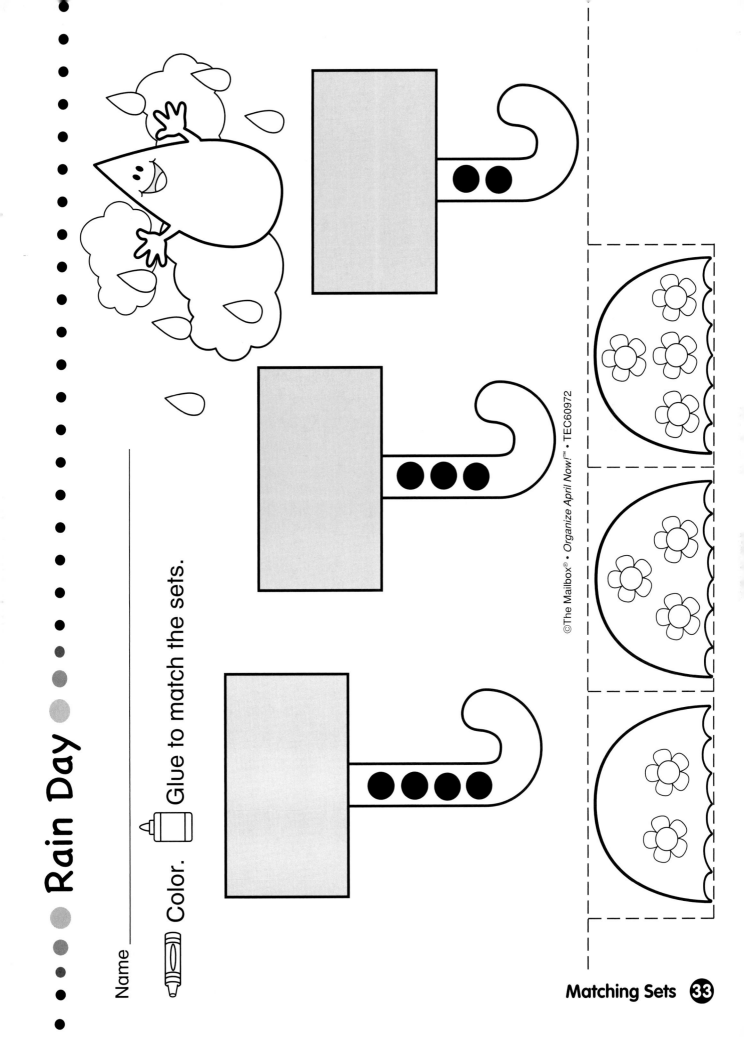

🖍 Color. 🧴 Glue to match the sets.

Pond

Eli's pond

Pond Pictures

Have each child cover a sheet of white paper with blue fingerpaint. When the paint is dry, direct him to tear a large, abstract pond shape from his paper. Next, help him glue it to a sheet of green construction paper. Encourage him to add several cattail stems with a thin black marker and then top each with a brown fingerprint. Complete each child's pond picture by personalizing it as shown.

Gone Fishin'

Casting around for a "fin-tastic" way to help youngsters learn to spell their names? Send them fishing! Cut a large pond from blue bulletin board paper and tape it to a tabletop. Program each of a supply of construction paper fish (patterns on page 38) with a different letter needed to spell each child's name. Spread the fish on the pond and store a set of student name cards nearby. A child finds her name card and places the fish that match the letters underneath. For an added challenge, have the child identify each letter as she matches the fish to her name card.

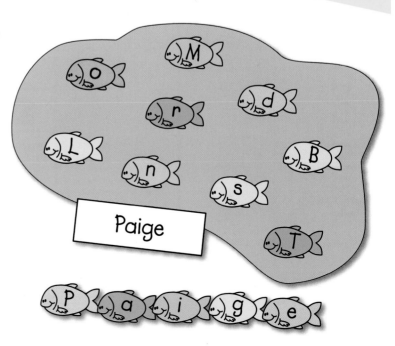

Paige

Splish, splash! This pond is full of perfectly preschool skills!

Patterns • • • • • • • • • • • • • • • • `Math`

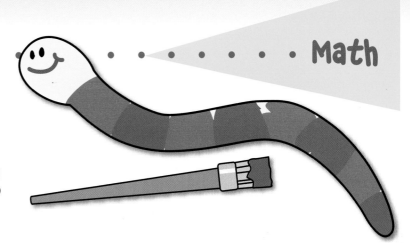

Stripes!

What pond creatures slither and slide? These snazzy striped snakes! Give each child a white construction paper snake cutout. Have him choose two colors of paint and then help him begin an AB pattern by painting alternating stripes. Encourage him to extend the pattern to completely decorate his snake.

Creative Arts • • • • • • • • • • • • • *Participate in song*

At the Pond

Divide your class into five groups and assign each group a different animal from the song shown. Teach each group its accompanying sound and motion. As you sing, point to each group, in turn, to act out its assigned animal.

(sung to the tune of "The Twelve Days of Christmas")

On the first day that I made a visit to the pond,
Frogs were jumping on logs. *Ribbit!*

On the second day that I made a visit to the pond,
Ducks were a-swimming. *Quack!*
And some frogs were jumping on logs. *Ribbit!*

On the third day that I made a visit to the pond,
Snakes slithered by. *Hiss!*
Ducks were a-swimming. *Quack!*
And some frogs were jumping on logs. *Ribbit!*

On the fourth day that I made a visit to the pond,
Crickets were singing. *Chirp!*
Snakes slithered by. *Hiss!*
Ducks were a-swimming. *Quack!*
And some frogs were jumping on logs. *Ribbit!*

On the fifth day that I made a visit to the pond,
I saw a fish! *Glub!*
Crickets were singing. *Chirp!*
Snakes slithered by. *Hiss!*
Ducks were a-swimming. *Quack!*
And some frogs were jumping on logs. *Ribbit!*

Lily Pad Numbers

With just a few touches, transform your water table into a miniature pond setting for a math center! Cut five green craft foam lily pads and label each with a different number from 1 to 5. Laminate and cut apart a green construction paper set of the frog manipulatives on page 38 and store them near the water table. A child in this center floats a lily pad in the water. Then he adds the corresponding number of frogs. He continues in this manner for each remaining lily pad.

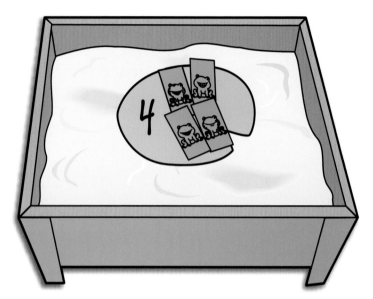

Gross-motor skills

Physical Health & Development

Froggy Says…

This splashy variation of Simon Says provides plenty of pond fun! To prepare, make a frog headband similar to the one shown. Have each child stand inside a personal pond (a plastic hoop or blue yarn circle laid on the floor). Put on the frog headband and give youngsters commands such as those shown. Then have a volunteer don the headband and take a turn giving Froggy's directions.

Hop like a frog.
Paddle like a turtle.
Hiss like a snake.
Swim like a fish.

Froggy says quack like a duck.

Who Lives at the Pond?

Youngsters show what they know about pond life at this classification center. Cut a large pond shape from blue construction paper; then mount it on a larger sheet of green paper. Color and cut out a copy of the animal cards on pages 39 and 40 and place them near the prepared pond workmat. A child in this center places the pond animals on the workmat and sets aside the animals who do not live at the pond.

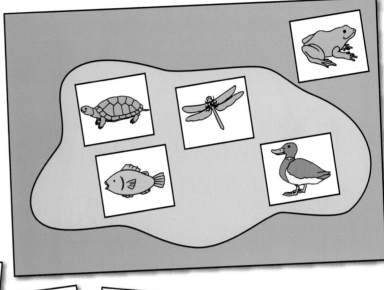

Math • • • • • • • • • • • • • • • • • • • Identifying colors

Rainbow Pond

Duplicate the pond animal cards on page 39 onto different rainbow colors of construction paper to make a class supply; then cut out the cards. Seat students in a circle and explain that they're going to an imaginary pond with unusually colored critters. Next, choose a volunteer to stand in the middle of the circle. Give each seated child a card and have him hold his card so that the blank side faces the volunteer. Chant the verse shown. The volunteer locates a card with the named color, identifies the animal, and exchanges places with the child holding it. Continue play in this manner for several rounds, changing the color each time.

Welcome to our pond!
What do you see?
Can you find a [green]
    critter for me?

Find a reproducible activity on page 41.

Fish Patterns

Use with "Gone Fishin'" on page 34.

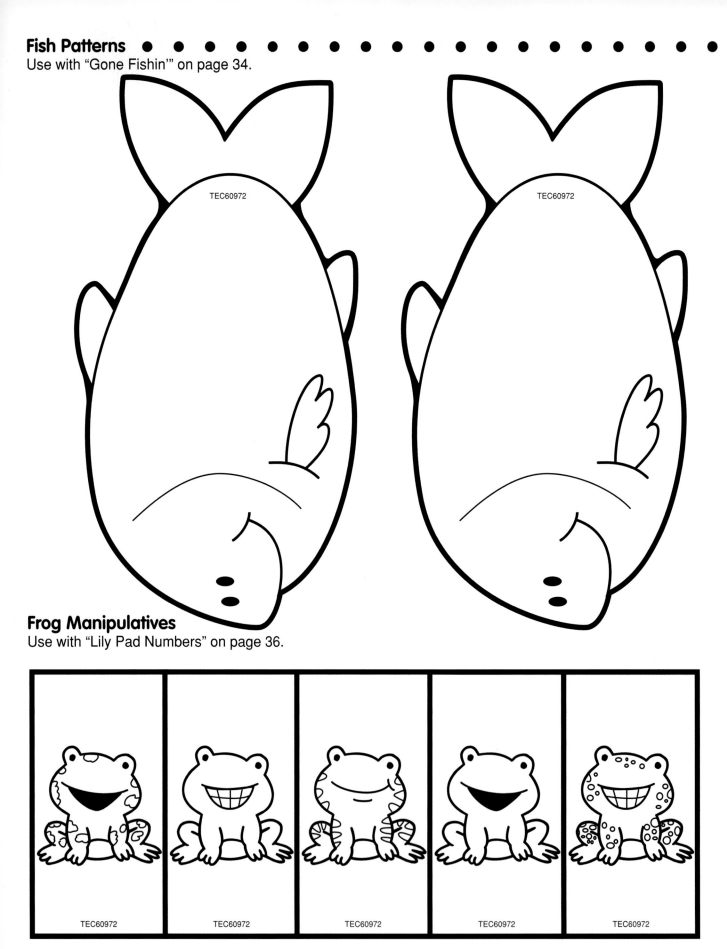

TEC60972

TEC60972

Frog Manipulatives

Use with "Lily Pad Numbers" on page 36.

TEC60972   TEC60972   TEC60972   TEC60972   TEC60972

TEC60972

TEC60972

TEC60972

TEC60972

TEC60972

TEC60972

TEC60972

TEC60972

TEC60972

TEC60972

TEC60972

TEC60972

What's on Turtle's Shell?

Name _____

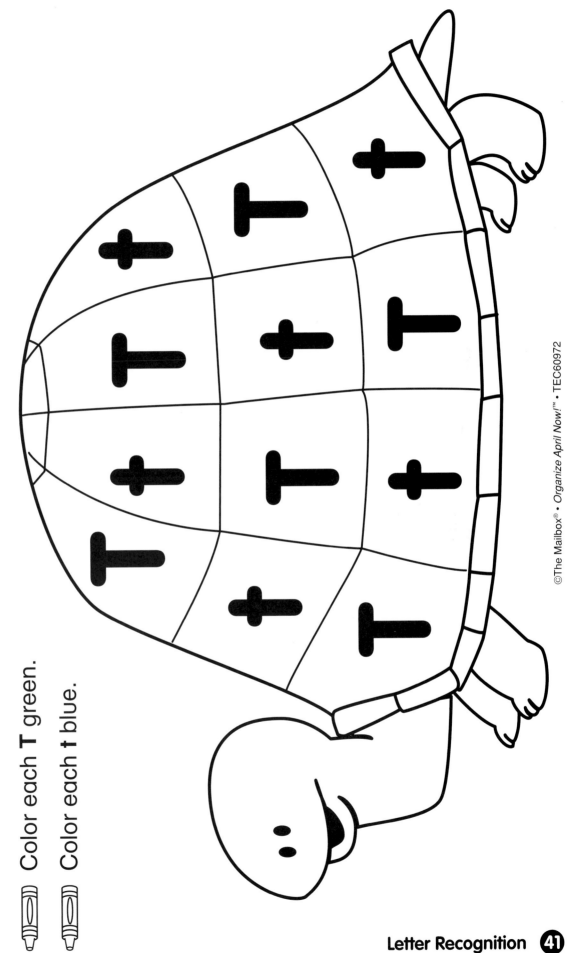

Color each T green.

Color each t blue.

Letter Recognition 41

Bunnies

Creative Arts

Mmm, Chocolate!

Little ones have a unique painting experience with this sweet project! Give each child a construction paper copy of the bunny pattern on page 46. Then place a dollop of chocolate pudding in the center of his paper. Have the youngster use his fingers to spread the pudding on the bunny until a desired effect is achieved. When the pudding is dry, cut out the bunny.

Rhyming

A Crop of Carrots

Color and cut out a copy of the cards on pages 47 and 48. Attach each large picture card to a separate basket (or other container). Place the carrots on a sheet of brown construction paper to resemble a garden and arrange the baskets nearby. Then gather a small group of children around the props. Have a child pretend to be a bunny and "pull" a carrot from the garden. Help her name the picture on the carrot and place it in the basket labeled with the rhyming picture. Continue with each student, in turn, until all the carrots have been placed in baskets.

Your little ones will be all ears for these cute-as-can-be learning opportunities all about bunnies.

A Bunny Bistro

Have little ones use their counting skills to make a pretend salad any bunny might enjoy! In advance, make a bowl cutout similar to the one shown for each child. Cut a cucumber, a carrot, and a large radish in half as shown. Place the halves at a table along with shallow pans of red, green, and orange tempera paint. Place a set of number cards nearby. To begin, gather a small group of youngsters at the table and give each child a bowl. Then hold up the number 3 and say, "Bunny would like three carrots in her salad." Have each child make three carrot prints in her bowl. Continue in the same way with the remaining vegetables, using a different number card each time.

Hiding in the Grass

Youngsters nestle cute little bunnies in the grass to keep them safe! To begin, place crinkled green paper shreds in your sensory table. Reduce the size of the bunny pattern on page 46. Then make several brown construction paper copies. Cut out the bunnies and place them near the sensory table. Explain to students that bunnies like to hide in tall grass or near bushes. Have each youngster, in turn, visit the center and tuck the bunnies in the grass.

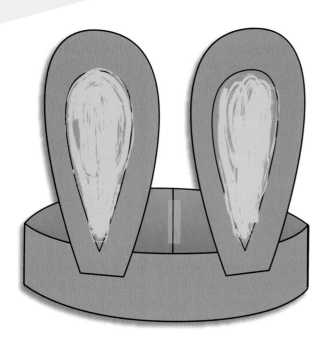

Listen Up!

Those big bunny ears sure are handy for hearing even the slightest sounds! Help each youngster make a simple bunny ear headband similar to the one shown. Then invite each child to don his headband and join you in your large-group area. Explain to students that bunnies have excellent hearing due to their very large ears. Encourage youngsters to pretend to be bunnies as they sit very quietly and listen. They might hear such sounds as the clock ticking, the ventilation system, or people walking outside the classroom. After a minute, have youngsters discuss what they heard.

Quiet Little Critters

In advance, make several construction paper copies of the bunny pattern on page 46. Cut out the bunnies and place them around your classroom so that they can be seen but not easily spotted. To begin, explain that bunnies are very quiet critters. Tell students that there are several quiet bunnies hiding in the classroom right now! Have youngsters scan the room. When a youngster spots a bunny, help him identify the bunny's location using a positional word, such as *under, over, below, beside,* or *on.* Then have the youngster pick up the bunny and bring it to you. Repeat the process with each bunny in the room, calling on a different child each time.

The bunny is under the chair!

The Bunny Hop

This twist on "The Hokey-Pokey" is sure to be a hit with your youngsters! Lead students in performing the song, encouraging them to shake their pretend cotton-tails after the final line. Then repeat the song three more times, each time substituting the underlined phrase with a different phrase (see the suggestions below) and a corresponding action.

(sung to the tune of "The Hokey-Pokey")

The bunnies hop right in.
The bunnies hop right out.
The bunnies hop right in.
'Cause hopping's what it's all about!
You do a little dance, and you're happy as can be.
Please [shake your tail] for me!

Suggested phrases: *twitch your nose, munch some grass, thump your feet*

Literacy • • • • • • • • • • • • • • • • • • • *Writing*

Oh So Soft

Bunny fur is very soft—and so are the projects in this nifty writing activity! Use the pattern on page 46 to make a construction paper bunny cutout for each child. Have each youngster spread glue on her bunny and then press cotton batting (or cotton balls) over the glue. Next, as each child pets her bunny, have her share the name of another object or animal that feels soft. Write each child's response on a sentence strip. Then display the bunnies and strips in the classroom.

The bunny feels soft, and my blanket feels soft.
Jackie

Find a reproducible activity on page 49.

Bunnies 45

Bunny Pattern

Use with "Mmm, Chocolate!" on page 42, "Hiding in the Grass" on page 43, "Quiet Little Critters" on page 44, and "Oh So Soft" on page 45.

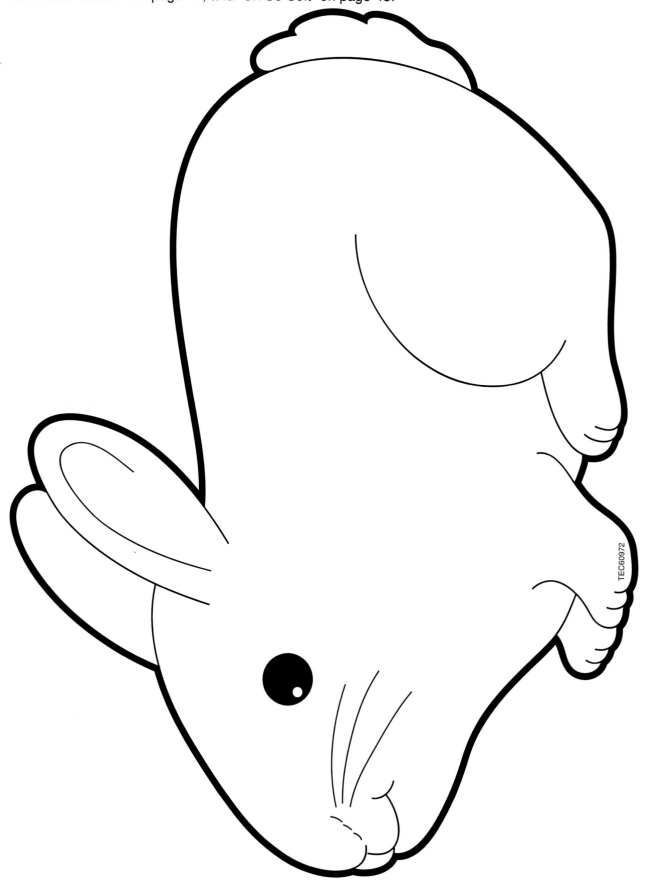

46 Bunnies

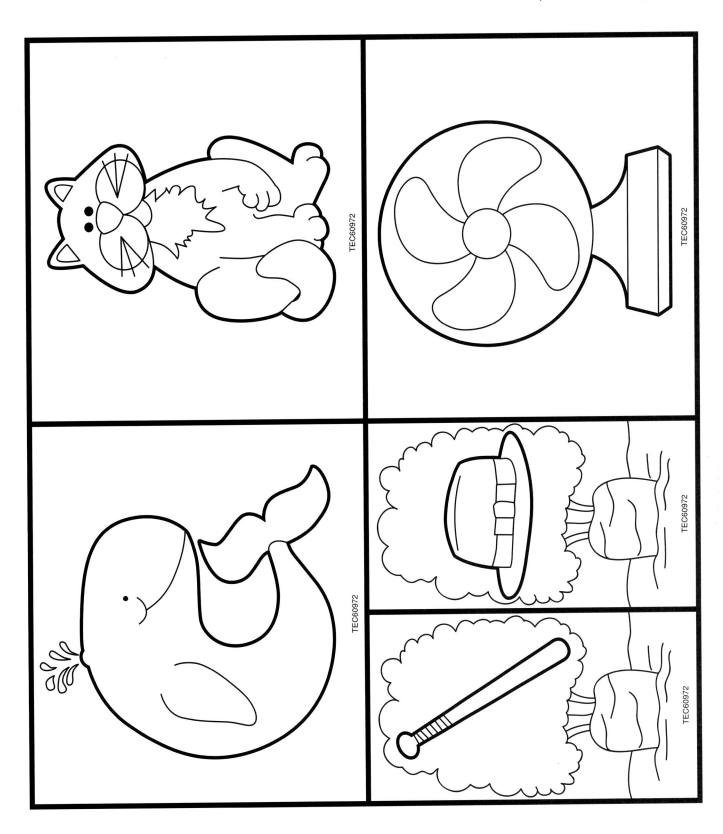

Carrot Cards

Use with "A Crop of Carrots" on page 42.

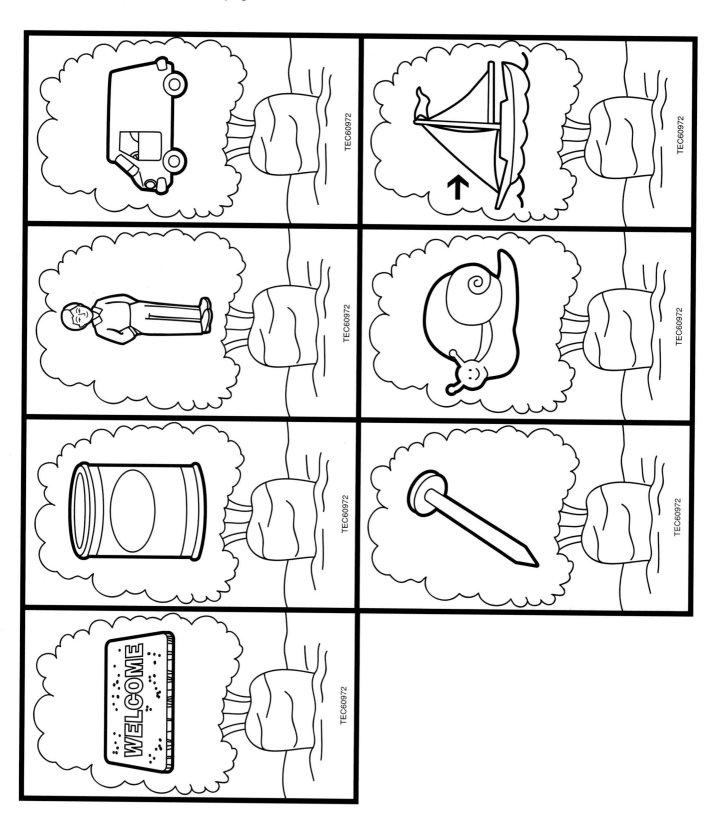

A Crunchy Crop

Name _____

✂ Cut.
Glue the pictures in order.

| 1 | 2 | 3 |

Arts & Crafts

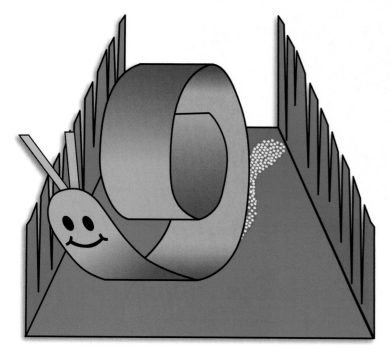

Snail Trail

This slow-moving critter leaves behind a glittery path! Fold in two sides of a four-inch green construction paper square so that the edges meet at the center. Unfold the sides and fringe-cut each side to resemble grass. To make a snail, round both corners at one end of a 1" x 9" construction paper strip. Draw a face and glue a pair of antennae on the rounded end. Next, roll the strip around a pencil, leaving the snail's head facing outward. Remove the snail from the pencil, and glue it to the middle of the grass. Squeeze a trail of glitter glue behind the snail, and allow the glue to dry. Then fold up the grass as shown.

Frogs on Logs

To make a frog, press two green thumbprints, one on top of the other, on a white paper strip as shown. Add two green pinkie prints at the top for eyes. Make several frogs in the same manner. When the paint is dry, glue brown paper strips under the frogs to resemble logs. Then use a fine-tip black marker to add details to the frogs and the logs. Color blue water and pond plants to complete the scene.

Teeny Turtle

A turtle and its pond home are the result of this project! To make a turtle, cut out a green construction paper copy of a turtle pattern on page 54. Cut off the bottom inch of a foam cup. Discard the top and paint the bottom green to represent a turtle shell. (Add a squirt of dishwashing liquid to the paint to help it stick to the cup.) After the paint is dry, glue the shell to the cutout. Use watercolors to paint a paper plate to resemble a pond. Allow time for the paint to dry. Then glue the turtle to its new home!

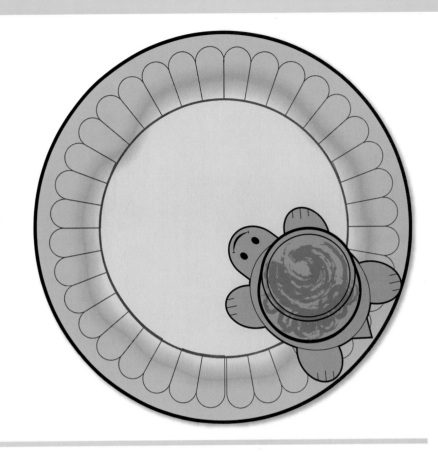

Rain, Rain, Go Away!

Turn a rainy scene into a sunny one with this idea! Draw a sunny outdoor picture on a sheet of construction paper, making sure to include a sun at the top of the page. Cut a sheet of waxed paper to match the size of the construction paper. Roll a round, plastic bristle hairbrush in blue paint and then on the waxed paper to create raindrops. After the paint is dry, staple the waxed paper atop the sunny scene. Finally, glue cotton ball clouds on the waxed paper so the sun is covered. Simply lift the waxed paper to make the rain go away!

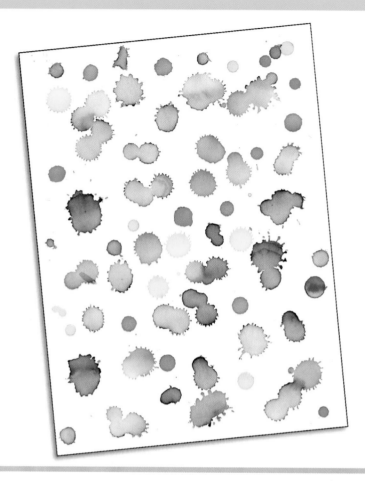

Drip Drop Raindrops

In advance, tint containers of water with red, yellow, and blue food coloring and place an eyedropper in each. To make a painting, use an eyedropper to drip colorful water (raindrops) on a sheet of white construction paper. Use each color to make several raindrops in the same way, allowing some of the raindrops to blend together to form new colors. If desired, cut the finished product into a raindrop shape.

Bunny Tails

What better way to make cute little bunnies than to use one of their favorite foods—carrots! To prepare a set of stampers, attach to separate plastic forks a large round carrot slice (body), a slightly smaller round carrot slice (head), and half of a length of a baby carrot (ears). To make a bunny, dip the body into brown paint and press it on a sheet of construction paper to make a print. Next, print a brown head and ears above the body. Make a few more bunnies in the same manner. When the paint is dry, use crayons to add a fence and grass. Glue a small piece of a cotton ball to each bunny to resemble a tail.

Peep Puppet

This sweet chick is awakening to celebrate spring! To prepare, cut out a white construction paper copy of the egg and nest patterns on page 55. Cut along the dotted line on the nest to make a slit. Pinch a craft feather in a spring-type clothespin to make a paintbrush. To make a chick, use the feather to paint the egg yellow. When the paint is dry, use markers to add eyes and a beak. Glue a craft feather to the top of the chick and attach a craft-stick handle to complete the puppet. To make a nest, color the pattern and glue on brown crinkled gift bag filler, leaving the slit uncovered. When the glue is dry, insert the chick's handle into the slit as shown; then slide the chick up and down behind the nest.

Elegant Egg

A crayon-resist technique makes an "eggs-traordinary" project! To make an egg, tape a sheet of white construction paper to a textured material, such as a wallpaper sample or a large doily. Firmly rub the side of an unwrapped white crayon over the paper. Then paint the paper with egg dye or with water tinted with food coloring. (The crayon will resist the paint and create a marbled effect.) After about one minute, blot the excess dye with a paper towel and set the project aside to dry. Then cut the completed painting into a large egg shape. If desired, frame the egg by gluing it to a colorful sheet of construction paper.

TEC60972

TEC60972

TEC60972

TEC60972

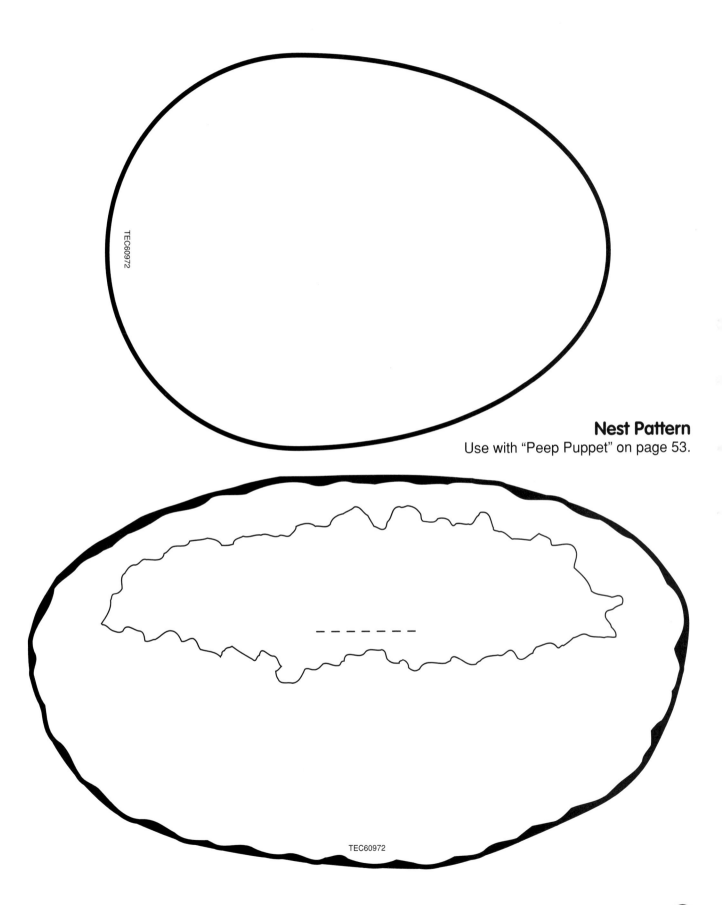

TEC60972

Nest Pattern
Use with "Peep Puppet" on page 53.

TEC60972

Bulletin Boards &

Grade A Attendance

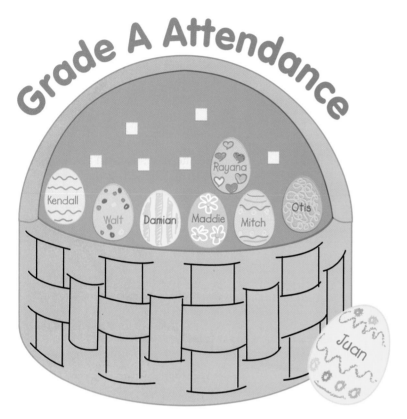

Draw a basket on a large sheet of bulletin board paper and cut it out. Glue the basket to a different-colored sheet of bulletin board paper and trim around the basket. For each student, attach the hook side of a Velcro fastener to the basket. Give each child a personalized tagboard egg cutout (pattern on page 55) to decorate. Attach the loop side of a Velcro fastener to the back of each egg. Mount the basket within students' reach, and place the eggs nearby. When a child arrives each day, he finds his egg and attaches it to the display.

Have each youngster spread brown fingerpaint on a green sheet of construction paper to resemble mud. Then invite her to use her fingers to draw a simple picture or write her name, a letter, or a number in the paint. After the paint is dry, help her cut her painting into a puddle shape. Display students' completed projects on a bulletin board along with a pig character (enlarge the pattern on page 58) and the title shown.

Displays

Recognize Earth Day with a display of recyclable goods! On a bulletin board, display a large recycling-bin character similar to the one shown. After a discussion about what can be recycled, help youngsters cut out pictures of appropriate items from magazines or store circulars. Display the items above the recycling bin and add the title shown.

Youngsters will be "hoppy" to see their names on this pond-inspired door display! Invite each child to use art materials to decorate a personalized frog cutout (patterns on page 59). Mount the frogs on a door covered with blue paper. Add lily pad cutouts and the title shown.

TEC60972

TEC60972

TEC60972

Centers

Creative Arts

Using art media

Funny Bunny

Little ones will hop right over to the art center to make this project! Stock a center with a supply of white, brown, and gray construction paper; cotton balls; and a variety of other art materials. Help a center visitor spread his fingers apart and trace his hand (excluding the thumb) on a sheet of paper in the color of his choice. Also trace his foot on the paper; then cut out both shapes. Have him glue the cutouts together to resemble a bunny. Encourage him to use the art materials to decorate his bunny and to add a cotton ball tail.

Letter formation

Literacy

Writing in the Water

To make a personal pond, squirt blue paint into a resealable plastic bag. Seal the bag and then secure it with packing tape. Place the bag and a set of letter cards at a center. A child chooses a letter card and then uses his fingers to write the letter on the pond. After he is satisfied with his writing, he rubs his hand over the bag to erase it; then he repeats the process with additional cards.

Gross-motor skills

Rain Dance

Make a raindrop by filling a blue sock with cotton balls and tying it closed. On a length of blue bulletin board paper, draw five puddle shapes and write a different numeral from 1 to 5 in each. Place the prepared paper and the raindrop at a center. A youngster tosses the raindrop onto the paper and announces the number in the puddle where the raindrop fell. Then he jumps, hops, skips, or claps the number to create a unique rain dance. He retrieves the raindrop and repeats the activity as time allows.

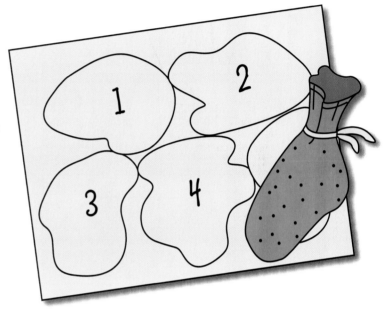

Math

One-to-one correspondence

Umbrella Repair Shop

Each umbrella at this center needs a handle! Copy and cut out several construction paper umbrellas (pattern on page 63). Cut off the handle from each umbrella. Place the umbrella tops and handles at a center. A visiting repair person places a handle on each umbrella top. For an added challenge, vary the number of handles at the center. Ask a center visitor to place a handle on each umbrella top and then use terms such as *more, less,* and *same* to describe the outcome.

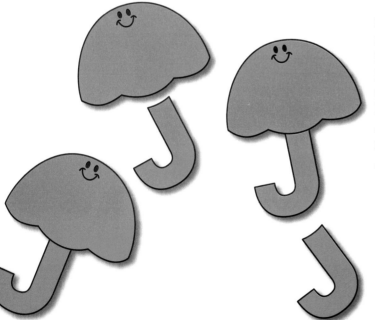

Literacy

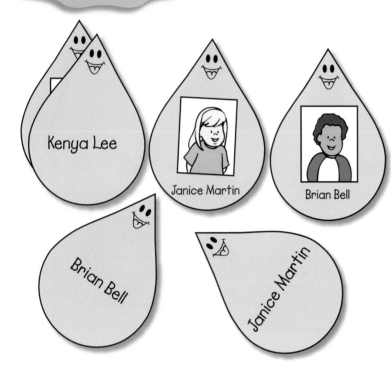

Shower of Friends

Preschoolers are sure to fall for this picture-perfect center! Cut out two construction paper raindrops (patterns on page 64) for each student. Write each child's name on a separate raindrop. Then, on each of the remaining raindrops, glue a student's photo and write her name. Place the raindrops at a center. A youngster spreads out the raindrops and matches each pair.

Kenya Lee

Janice Martin

Brian Bell

Brian Bell

Janice Martin

Number sets

Math

Pond Parade

This partner center is just ducky! To prepare, cut out several brown duck prints and a yellow and a white construction paper duck using the patterns on page 65. Also cut out a large blue paper pond. Label one duck print "Start." Then tape the pond and duck prints to the floor at a center as shown. Place the ducks and a jumbo die nearby.

To begin, each child chooses a duck and places it on "Start." The first player rolls the die and moves his duck the corresponding number of spaces along the duck prints. Students take turns in this manner until both ducks circle the pond.

TEC60972

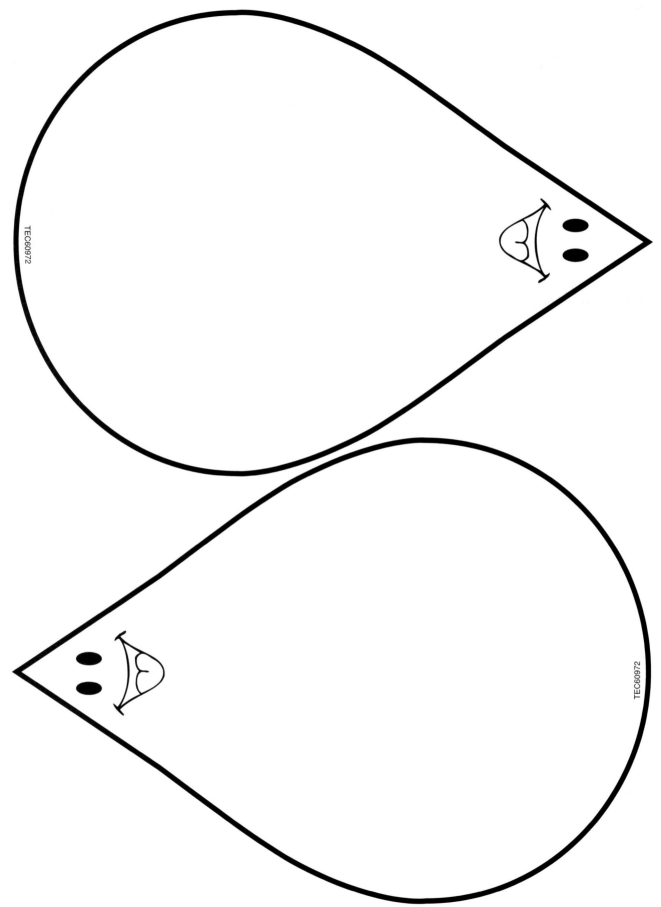

TEC60972

TEC60972

TEC60972

TEC60972

TEC60972

Circle Time & Games

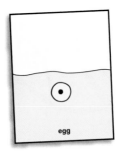

Science

Exploring living things

From Egg to Frog

Acting out each stage of a frog's life is a great way for your preschoolers to get their wiggles out! Color and cut out a construction paper copy of the life stages cards on page 68. Gather youngsters and display one card at a time, encouraging them to discuss what they see. Then, as you point to each card, invite little ones to perform a corresponding movement (see suggestions shown).

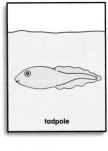

egg

tadpole

froglet

frog

Movements

egg: lay on the floor in a balled-up position

tadpole: lay straight on the floor with arms flat against your body and wiggle around

froglet: wiggle around on the floor moving arms and legs

frog: hop around using legs and arms

Physical Health & Development

Gross-motor skills

Puddle Play

Gather students in a circle around an imaginary puddle. Then lead little ones in the song shown. Have students move as indicated around the circle as they sing. At the end of the verse, invite youngsters to sink down into the puddle.

(sung to the tune of "Ring Around the Rosie")

[Walk] around the puddle.
Lots and lots of water
Splashes, splashes.
We all get wet!

Repeat, substituting one of the following action words for each subsequent verse: *jump, march, skip, tiptoe.*

Following directions

Bunnies Hop, Bunnies Stop

Here's a springtime game that will get your little ones moving! To prepare, label a large red egg cutout "stop" and a large green egg cutout "go." Have each youngster color a copy of one of the bunny patterns on page 69, cut it out, and glue it on a construction paper strip. Size each student's strip to form a headband and secure the ends. Invite each child to don her headband.

To play, line up youngsters side by side in an open area of the classroom or outside. Stand several feet away from the line. When you hold up the green egg, say, "Bunnies hop!" and encourage little ones to hop toward you. When you hold up the red egg, say, "Bunnies stop!" and have youngsters freeze. Continue alternating between the eggs until your little bunnies have hopped all the way to you!

Math

Counting

In the Basket

Little ones will enjoy collecting eggs and singing this catchy tune! For each child, cut off the top half of a paper lunch bag and discard it. Invite each student to decorate her bag. Open the bag bottom and staple on a construction paper handle to resemble a basket. In an open area, spread out a large supply of plastic eggs or egg cutouts. Lead youngsters in the song shown. While singing, each child picks up one egg at a time and places it in her basket. After the end of the verse, youngsters stop; count their eggs; and, in turn, announce their numbers to the class. Then have little ones return their eggs to the floor for another round of play!

(sung to the tune of "Pawpaw Patch")

Pick up an egg and put it in your basket.
Pick up an egg and put it in your basket.
Pick up an egg and put it in your basket.
Stop! How many eggs do you have?

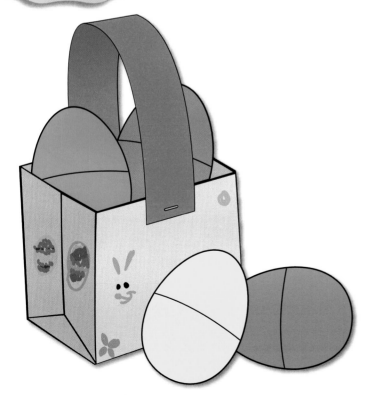

egg

TEC60972

tadpole

TEC60972

froglet

TEC60972

frog

TEC60972

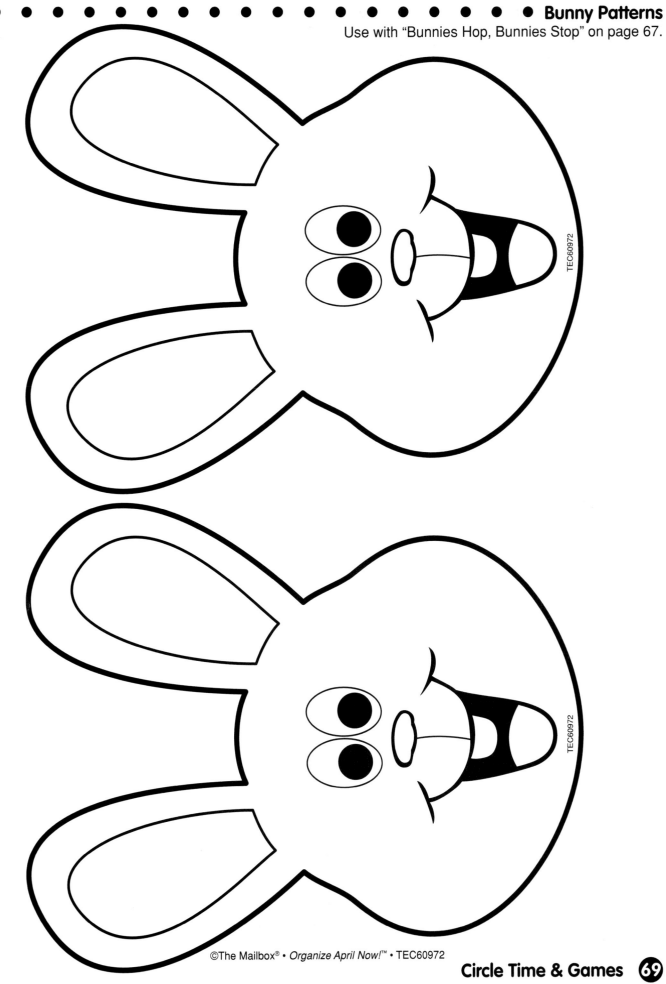

TEC60972

TEC60972

Management Tips

Choice Eggs

Get little ones involved in choosing a class activity with this "egg-cellent" idea. Write a different movement idea or song title on each of several slips of paper. Place each slip inside a different plastic egg; then put the eggs in a basket. At group time, invite a child to open an egg. Read the slip aloud and then lead little ones in doing the activity or singing the song.

Hop like a bunny.

"Ten-Carrot" Behavior!

Helping a little bunny collect carrots encourages youngsters' good behavior. Display a simple paper plate bunny face. Make five copies of page 71. Color and cut out the carrot patterns and place them in a container near the bunny display. Tell youngsters that their good behavior will help the bunny collect all ten of his carrots. Each time your group follows a classroom rule, announce that they have earned a carrot as you tape it on the display. When the class has earned all ten carrots, reward them with a special treat or privilege.

TEC60972

TEC60972

Busy Frogs

Little ones pretend to be frogs with this "hoppy" tune! Encourage youngsters to perform the indicated action as you sing the song. Then repeat the song, substituting other action words, such as *dancing, croaking,* and *sleeping.*

(sung to the tune of "The Muffin Man")

Oh look! I see some [hopping] frogs,
Some [hopping] frogs, some [hopping] frogs.
Oh look! I see some [hopping] frogs,
[Hopping] around the pond.

Little Bird-Watchers

This calm poem encourages youngsters to quietly observe our fine-feathered friends.

There are white eggs and brown eggs
And speckled ones too.
There are big ones and small ones,
And some are bright blue.
Eggs are kept safe
In nests warm and dry.
They hatch into babies
That learn to fly!

Fingerplays

Springtime Bunnies

Twitch, wiggle, hop—moving like a bunny is sure to get youngsters excited about springtime!

I saw a small brown bunny.
Do you think he saw me?
He wiggled his furry tail,
Then hopped behind a tree.

Put hands on top of head for bunny ears.
Point to self.
Move hips side to side.
Hop in a circle.

He peeked out from behind that tree
And twitched his little pink nose.
Then off he hopped into the field
On his little bunny toes.

Place hands over eyes.
Wiggle nose.
Hop around room.
Hop around room.

Happy Earth Day!

Celebrate Earth Day as youngsters think about keeping the earth clean.

(sung to the tune of "Twinkle, Twinkle, Little Star")

Our big earth is really great!
Now it's time to celebrate.
Think of things that we can do
To keep our water clean and blue.
Help our land stay bright and green.
Let's not litter—keep Earth clean!

Bunny's Crop

A ready-to-use center mat and cards

Materials:

center mat to the right
center cards on pages 77 and 79
resealable plastic bag

Preparing the center:

Cut out the cards and place them in the bag.

Using the center:

1. A child removes the cards from the bag and sorts them by vegetable (carrot or lettuce).

2. He chooses a carrot card, counts the carrots, and then finds the lettuce card with the same number of vegetables.

3. To check his work, he turns over the two cards. If the colored dots match, he places the cards on the mat. If not, he turns the cards over and searches for the correct card to make a matching pair. When he finds the card, he places both cards on the mat.

4. He repeats Steps 2 and 3 until all the cards are placed on the mat.

Family Follow-Up

After a youngster completes the center activity, have him take home a copy of page 81 to complete with a parent.

74 Bunny's Crop

Bunny's Crop

Match.
Put.

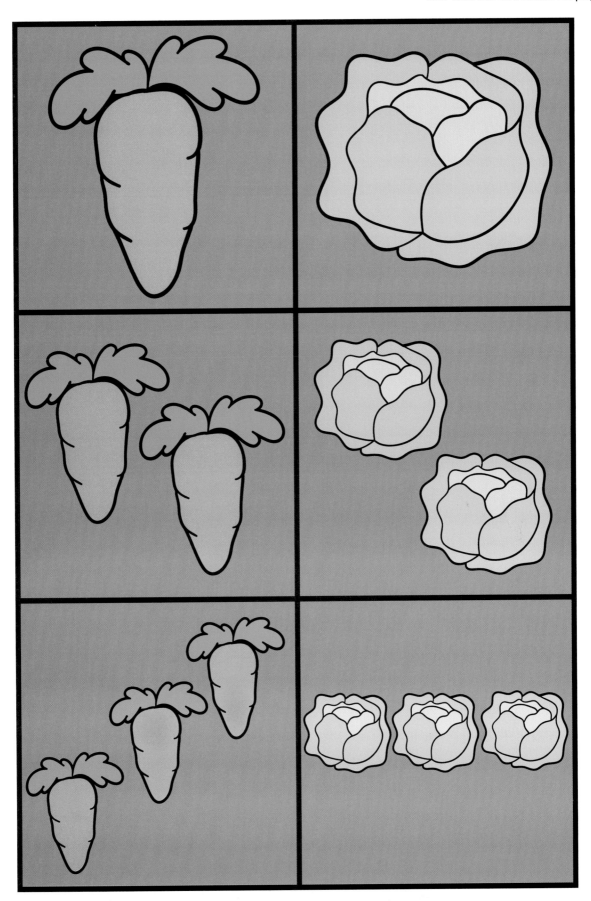

Bunny's Crop
TEC60972

Bunny's Crop
TEC60972

Bunny's Crop
TEC60972

Bunny's Crop
TEC60972

Bunny's Crop
TEC60972

Bunny's Crop
TEC60972

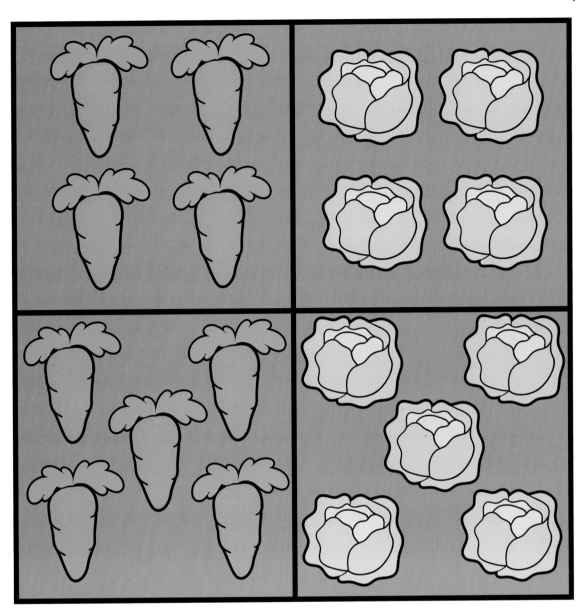

Bunny's Crop
TEC60972

Bunny's Crop
TEC60972

Bunny's Crop
TEC60972

Bunny's Crop
TEC60972

Dear Parent,
  We have been practicing counting. Help your child count the carrots shown.

A Rainy Day

A ready-to-use center mat and cards

Materials:

center mat to the right
center cards on pages 85 and 87
resealable plastic bag

Preparing the center:

Cut out the cards and put them in the bag.

Using the center:

1. A child removes the cards from the bag and places each one green side up in the center area.
2. She chooses a card and names the picture.
3. She decides whether the picture's name begins with the /r/ sound like the beginning sound in the word *rain.* If it does, she places the card on the mat. If it does not, she places it in a separate pile.
4. She repeats Steps 2 and 3 for each card.
5. To check her work, she turns over the stack of cards on the center mat. If each card in the stack has the same picture on the back, she proceeds to Step 6. If not, she turns the cards over and rearranges them until they are sorted correctly; then she proceeds to Step 6.
6. She says the name of the picture on each card from the mat, emphasizing the /r/ sound at the beginning of each word.

Family Follow-Up

After a youngster completes the center activity, have her take home a copy of page 89 to complete with a parent.

A Rainy Day

Say.
Put.

A Rainy Day
TEC60972

A Rainy Day
TEC60972

A Rainy Day
TEC60972

A Rainy Day
TEC60972

A Rainy Day
TEC60972

A Rainy Day
TEC60972

A Rainy Day
TEC60972

A Rainy Day
TEC60972

A Rainy Day
TEC60972

A Rainy Day
TEC60972

A Rainy Day
TEC60972

A Rainy Day
TEC60972

Dear Parent,
    We have been listening for the sound of the letter *r*. Help your child say the name of each picture below and decide whether it begins with the /r/ sound. Then ask your child to color the pictures that begin with the /r/ sound.

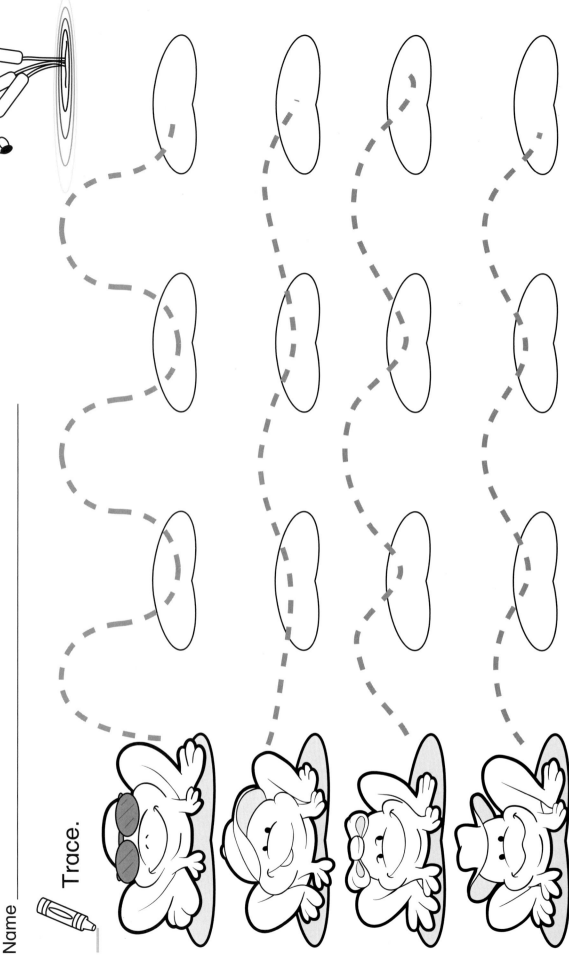

Lily Pad Leaping

Name _____

Trace.

Tracing

Yummy Jelly Beans

Name _____

 Color. Cut. Glue.

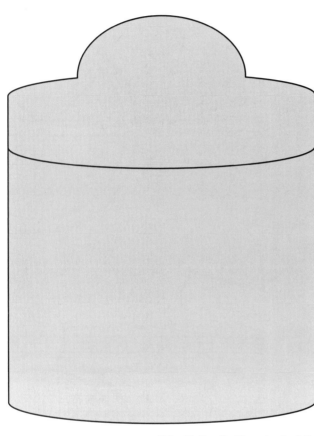

©The Mailbox® • *Organize April Now!*™ • TEC60972

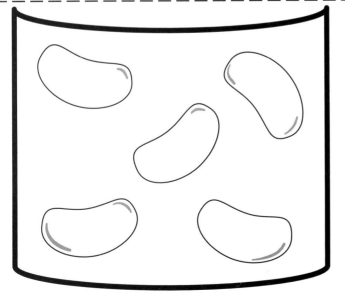

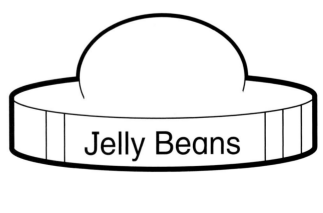

Jelly Beans

96 **Cut and Glue**

"Wheely" Fun Ride!

Name _____

🖍 Color.

✂ Cut.

🍶 Glue.

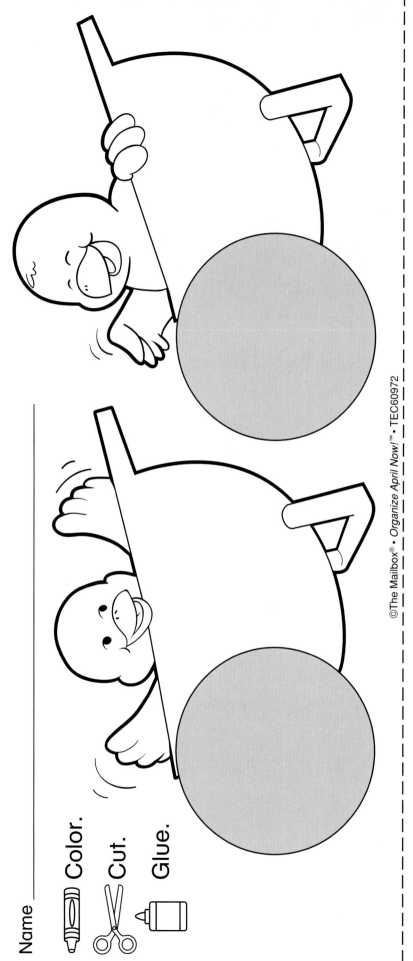

©The Mailbox® • *Organize April Now!*™ • TEC60972

Staying Dry

Name _____

🖍 Color.

✂️ Cut.

🧴 Glue.

©The Mailbox® • *Organize April Now!*™ • TEC60972

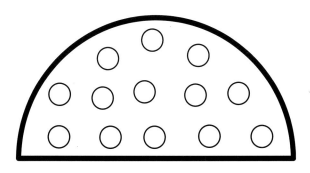

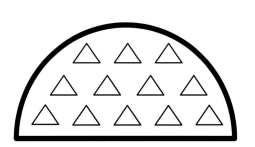

94 **Cut and Glue**

Flying Over Flowers

Name _____

Color.

Cut.

Glue.

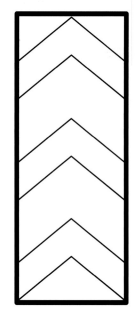

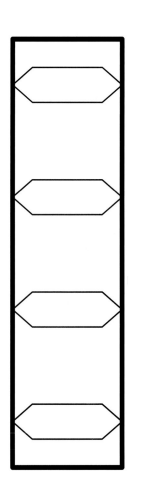

©The Mailbox® • *Organize April Now!*™ • TEC60972

Name _____

Trace.

Color.

Rainbow Painting

Name _____

Trace.

Color.